Hibernation

by Tori Kosara

SCHOLASTIC INC.

New York   Toronto   London   Auckland
Sydney   Mexico City   New Delhi   Hong Kong

ISBN 978-0-545-36582-6

12 11 10   15 16/0
Printed in the U.S.A.   40
                    First printing, November 2011

Every year, when winter rolls in, it is too cold for many animals to live comfortably. Food also becomes difficult to find. Many animals, such as birds, migrate (MYE-grayt) to warmer places. Other animals stay put and sleep through the cold season. This is called hibernation (HYE-bur-nay-shun).

When an animal is ready to hibernate, it looks for a warm, safe place, such as a cave or a burrow to curl up in for the winter.

These areas are well-protected from harsh winter weather and keep animals safe from predators. Animals settle into these safe spots, and fall into a deep sleep.

CHIPMUNK

Some hibernators, such as woodchucks, chipmunks, hedgehogs, and bats sleep so deeply that they may appear to be dead.

Their breathing and heart rates drop to very low levels, and it is difficult to wake them. These types of hibernators are called true hibernators.

HEDGEHOG

BEAR

Other hibernators, such as bears and raccoons, are lighter sleepers during the winter months.

They can be woken up easily, and they sometimes come out from their sleeping place to look for food or water. A short period of hibernation like this is called torpor.

Before cuddling up for winter, hibernators try to eat a lot because many of them don't eat at all during hibernation. Even the lighter sleepers that can wake up eat very little.

Much of the food animals eat to prepare for hibernation is stored as fat. This helps them to sleep through winter without eating much or anything at all. The extra fat gives them all the nutrients and energy they need to survive while asleep.

CHIPMUNK

The food they eat helps the animals to store brown fat. This thick extra layer of fat is special because it helps to keep the animals warm.

CHIPMUNK

Brown fat makes heat, which helps to protect a hibernating animal's organs, such as the brain, while it sleeps through the cold winter.

A special substance in the animals' blood tells them when it's time to store up food, search for a shelter, and, finally, go to sleep.

BEAR

The normal body temperature of most warm-blooded animals is between 97° F (36° C) and 109° F (43° C).

DORMOUSE

The body temperature of a true hibernator, however, drops to about 32° F (0° C) while it sleeps. That is the same temperature at which water freezes! Luckily, the animal's brown fat keeps it warm enough to survive the cold temperatures.

A woodchuck is a true hibernator. Woodchucks' teeth are constantly growing. They grow so fast that woodchucks have to gnaw on their food just to wear them down. But during hibernation, a woodchuck's teeth stop growing, which is lucky because it does not eat!

Bats are true hibernators that must find a shelter that stays above freezing all winter.

A cave where bats or other hibernating animals gather is called a hibernaculum (hye-bur-NA-kyoo-lum).

Some cold-blooded animals, such as frogs and toads, bury themselves in mud while they are hibernating.

The mud keeps them warm
and safe until spring.

Snakes also hibernate. They like to stay together to keep themselves extra warm.

They like to sleep in places such as beneath rocks or in other burrows.

Unlike most fish, Antarctic cod enter a hibernation-like state during the winter.

Like other true hibernators, the fishes' heart rates slow down. Unlike other hibernators, these fish rest on the seafloor until the spring sun returns.

Estivation (es-ti-VAY-shun) is similar to hibernation. During long periods of very high temperatures or drought, some animals, like snails and crocodiles, estivate in order to survive.

The animals find a safe place to rest, they eat little to no food, and their heart and breathing rates slow down.

SNAIL

After several weeks of hibernation, animals wake slowly because they have very little energy. Luckily, the fat they've stored gives them just enough energy to search for more food.

BEAR

SQUIRREL

The animals will then eat and sleep normally until the next year when they must prepare for another long season of hibernation.

Glossary

Burrow: a hole in the ground that is used for protection by an animal

Cold-blooded: having a body temperature that changes according to the temperature of the surroundings

Drought: dry weather that lasts for a long period of time

Estivation: a state in which an animal has a low heart and breathing rate and low intake of food as it rests during a long period of drought

Hibernaculum: a cave in which animals hibernate

Hibernation: a state in which an animal has a low heart and breathing rate and low intake of food as it rests during the winter

Migrate: to move from one place to another

Organ: a part of an animal, made of tissues and cells, that performs a special function

Predator: an animal that hunts other animals for food

Torpor: a shortened period of hibernation in which an animal is able to wake easily and move around

True Hibernators: hibernators that are difficult to wake

Warm-blooded: having a body temperature that does not change, even if the temperature is very hot or very cold